# WALKS IN OXFORDSHIRE

# Walks
# in Oxfordshire

**NIGEL HAMMOND**

SPURBOOKS LIMITED

*Published by*
**SPURBOOKS LIMITED**
*6 Parade Court*
*Bourne End*
*Buckinghamshire*

© SPURBOOKS LTD. 1977

Sketch Maps by Mike Pocock

I S B N  0  904978 25 7

# Contents

# Introduction

THE routes of the walks detailed here, take in some of the most scenic and best countryside of the new county of Oxfordshire. In the north of the area the stone villages of the Sibfords look into Warwickshire over the ancient drove road called Ditchedge Lane. Wide views over the Evenlode valley and Wychwood Forest, then to the Cotswolds, can be had in the area of Charlbury and Taston.

Contrasting countryside, Otmoor and the Cherwell valley, can be walked in the area of Tackley, Kirtlington and Charlton-on-Otmoor, while if it is history you want, then take the walks from Woodstock to Blenheim.

A wide variety of countryside exists in the Vale of the White Horse, an area of Oxfordshire which has been recently transferred from Berkshire. Walk along the Thames at Abingdon or near Wittenham Clumps and maybe in the Fyfield to Northmoor area. Alternatively you may wish to sample the quiet of the pastureland in the depth of the Vale in the neighbourhood of the Hanneys and Charney Bassett.

My own favourite walks are around the Hanneys and across the Thames from Fyfield to Northmoor and Bablockhythe, but all are enjoyable, and will give you much pleasure in this splendid part of England.

NIGEL HAMMOND

7

# Area 1

**Sibford Ferris, Traitor's Ford, Ditchedge Lane, Sibford Gower — 4, 5 or 6 miles**

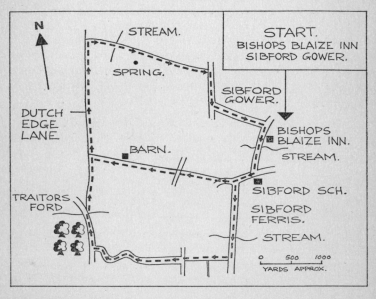

**How to get there:** By road using B4035 from Banbury or A34 from Oxford to Chipping Norton, thence by unclassified roads to Sibford Gower, where the walks begin and end.

**Refreshments: The Bishop's Blaize Inn,** Sibford Gower.

**What to see:** Some extremely picturesque and hilly countryside on the Oxfordshire-Warwickshire border which affords wide views over the upper Stour valley; the thatch and stone-built villages of Sibford Gower and Sibford Ferris; Ditchedge Lane, which is one of the ancient Drover's Roads of England.

8

## 4 mile walk

Start at **Bishop's Blaize Inn,** Sibford Gower. You walk sharply downhill then uphill to Sibford Ferris. At Sibford School turn right and walk straight on. Within 200 yards you will come to a road junction, but again walk straight ahead. Sibford House lies beyond the road junction, and 50 yards further on from the house you will find a grass track which runs straight ahead as the metalled road bears left. Take this grass track and cross two field gates. Beyond the second field gate leave the hedgerow gradually to your left and make for the far right-hand corner of the field. Cross the road and take the farm track which runs sharply uphill opposite. The track ends with a barn on your right, and becomes a footpath, continuing its original line over a field. At the second gate along the footpath, turn right into Ditchedge Lane for about a mile.

This lane was a broad track, used as a Drove Road, and as such forms one of the ancient routes of England, leading from the Chipping Norton area, circling to the north of Banbury and leads into the cattle pastures and market towns of Leicestershire. The portion of Ditchedge Lane which you are using marks the boundary between Oxfordshire and Warwickshire.

Equidistant between two prominent field barns which you will see on your right, turn off Ditchedge Lane to the right along a track which descends sharply. You will soon cross a gated bridge, then follow a hedgerow on your right equally sharply uphill. In 200 yards you cross a gate with a splendidly cool spring to your right. Walk straight on beside the walled garden of Home Farm, and on to the metalled road at Sibford Gower. Turn right, then left, along the village streets, and 150 yards beyond the church turn right again to regain the **Bishop's Blaize Inn,** where you started the walk.

## 5 mile walk

From **Bishop's Blaize Inn** walk to Sibford School turning right opposite the school, but at the second junction in 200 yards turn left and continue downhill. The road crosses a stream then ascends again. In 300 yards from the bridge a footpath crosses the line of the road, turn right on to it, passing a track to the left which leads to Belle Isle Farm. In some 450 yards the footpath meets a road junction, go straight on along the road until the next junction, then turn right.

Walking downhill through woodland, you are again on the line of Ditchedge Lane. A narrow footbridge will take you dry-footed over Traitor's Ford. The path you take along Ditchedge Lane leaves the road to the right immediately after the ford, and winds steeply uphill along the side of a field. Just short of the point where Ditchedge Lane changes from a footpath to a lane bordered by hedgerows, take a gate to the right and follow the route straight ahead to Sibford Ferris. At the road, cross over and aim for the high right-hand corner of the field opposite, where the hedgerow will be on your right. From here it is a straightforward walk along the footpath into Sibford Ferris which is a few hundred yards away.

## 6 mile walk

From **Bishop's Blaize Inn** follow the five mile walk to the gate which turned off Ditchedge Lane as described above. From this point follow Ditchedge Lane as described in the four mile walk.

# Area 2

**Charlbury, Taston, Clarke's Bottom, Stonesfield**

**3, 6 or 9 miles**

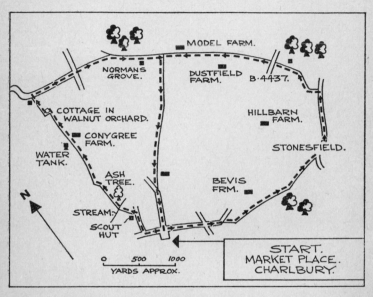

**How to get there:** By car using the B4022 from Witney; the B4437 from Woodstock; the B4026 from Chipping Norton. By rail to Charlbury station or by bus from Chipping Norton or Witney.

**Refreshments:** The **White Horse** at Stonesfield, or the **Bull, Bear** or **Rose and Crown** at Charlbury.

**What to see:** Stone-built villages on the base of the Cotswold dip slope; the small market town of Charlbury; slate quarries at Stonesfield and several wide views over the Cotswolds and Wychwood Forest.

## 3 mile walk

The walks can conveniently be started at Charlbury, where there is plenty of car parking space, and for the three mile walk you leave the market place by way of the B4026 towards Spelsbury. Follow Market Street, passing the White Hart on the right in Thames Street. Turn right up Nine Acres Lane, and in 200 yards take a footpath to the left beside the Charlbury Scout building.

Initially, head for a dominant ash tree in the valley bottom ahead. There is a stepping stone over a stream, and a stile. Head up the opposite slope, and half way along the hedge, which will appear to your right, is a stile into the next field. Walk to the top left corner of the field which you have entered, where you will find a gate and fence. Crossing them, turn left along the edge of the field, keeping the hedge to your left, in the depth of which is a lane now too overgrown to follow. At the end of the field, pass through an arch in the hedge and bear to the right.

A watertank will appear on the skyline, slightly to your left, head for it down the field boundary. Superb views are to be seen to your left over the Cotswolds, and back to Wychwood behind you.

Bear left at the Dutch Barns, and beyond, to the left of Conygree Farm, heading for the cottage at the far end of the pasture set in a fine walnut orchard. At the cottage turn sharply left and right. Taston village is ahead, and the metalled road is approached along a lane.

Turn right on to the road and walk uphill to the Enstone road. Cross the main road taking the narrow lane opposite to the corner of Shilcott Wood. You are now walking part of an ancient Drove Road, which in the opposite direction, extends round Chipping Norton and Banbury into the cattle pastures of Leicestershire.

Follow the lane past the cottage at Norman's Grove, and within half a mile turn right along a path which leads deeply into the valley of Clarke's bottom. Houses increase in frequency as one enters Charlbury, and the market place is a short distance ahead.

## 6 mile walk

From Charlbury market place turn right along the road out of the town towards Fawler and Finstock. At the edge of the town take the B4437 for 200 yards. Where the road turns left carry on ahead along a track which soon bears right. The path will take you to Stonesfield. To your right are views over the Evenlode valley extending to Cornbury Park and the Wychwood Forest, which may be seen through the high hedges which enclose the pathway. Soon the path opens out and descends, crossing the top of a wooded valley which runs down to the right. Curving up the opposite side of the valley the track quickly rises and levels, gradually descending into Stonesfield.

Turn left through the village taking the road running north from the village. At the end of the scatter of settlement some 400 yards from the village, a prominent track bears left from the line of the road.

Follow the track, which runs slightly downhill towards Sheer's Copse. Great care is necessary in selecting the correct path at the south west corner of Sheer's Copse. Keep the farm to your right. It is all too easy to take the left turn and find oneself walking back to Stonesfield. In fact, you should turn slightly right alongside a field hedgerow, which in a few hundred yards comes out on the B4437.

Cross the road with care. The track soon widens dramatically and you are on the major Drove Road used in the 18th and early 19th centuries, the continuation of which is detailed in the 3 mile walk.

Gently ascending towards Dustfield Farm, the track levels out. On the the right you pass lodges marking the private road into Ditchley Park. At the right time of year massive patches of bluebells border the track in the pheasant reservations to the right. Shortly after passing the Model Farm, take the footpath to the left along Clarke's Bottom, and using the 3 mile walk itinerary, complete the walk into Charlbury.

## 9 mile walk

This walk is an amalgamation of the 3 and 6 mile walks

taking the paths which pass round the circumference of them. It is best tackled starting from Charlbury and initially following the 6 mile walk to the top of Clarke's Bottom, then continuing by using the 3 mile walk in reverse through Taston to Charlbury.

# Area 3

**Tackley, Northbrook, Kirtlington, the Oxford Canal**

**4, 5½ or 8½ miles**

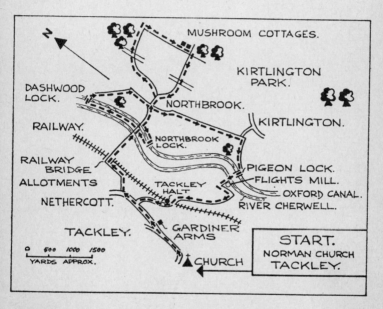

**How to get there:** British Railways from Banbury or Oxford to Tackley Halt. Oxford Omnibus services between Oxford, Woodstock and Banbury. By car, using A423 Oxford to Banbury road.

**Refreshments: Gardiner Arms,** Tackley; **Kings Arms,** Nethercott or the **Dashwood Arms** at Kirtlington.

**What to see:** Some typical Oxfordshire stone-built villages in Tackley and Kirtlington; Kirtlington Park; the Oxford Canal and the Cherwell valley.

## 4 mile walk

Take the Norman church at Tackley as your starting point. Follow the road which leads through this unspoilt village. Immediately after the church lies Tackley Park, on the right. At the village green take the right hand fork, passing the **Gardiner Arms** on the right.

After 500 yards you will arrive at the **King's Arms.** Continue straight on. In 100 yards the metalled road turns sharp left. The track you require rises in front of you at this turn, and is flanked by village allotments on the left. In just over 200 yards the rough stone track turns left and runs parallel with the railway but becomes increasingly grass covered as you progress.

Half-a-mile ahead the track turns right and crosses the railway by way of a black metal bridge. From this point is a splendid view over the Cherwell valley with the honey-coloured stone double-bridge (Northbrook Bridge) some 600 yards away which takes the track over the river and the Oxford Canal. You follow the footpath beside the hedgerow across the flood plain of the Cherwell to this bridge.

Cross Northbrook Bridge and turn right to Northbrook Lock. Cross over the canal and turn left along the towing path for a good mile-and-a-half to Pigeon Lock. Shortly before you reach Pigeon Lock, the considerable stone workings and the canal wharf at Kirtlington Quarries will be passed on your left. At Pigeon Lock continue the walk to Tackley as outlined in the 5½ mile walk.

## 5½ mile walk

Follow the 4 mile walk to Northbrook Bridge. From Northbrook canal bridge, turn right along the far side of the canal to Northbrook Lock, crossing the canal to the towing path which lies isolated between the canal and the Cherwell. Turn right along the path. In half-a-mile you will come to Dashwood Lock. Cross the canal by bridge 209 and within 15 yards take the gate on the right by a solitary oak tree. Cross the field in front of you aiming for the left corner of the wood. Pass through two gates at the side of the wood, then follow the gravel road to Northbrook.

At Northbrook you may return to Tackley by way of the canal path (see 4 mile walk) or by way of Kirtlington. For the Kirtlington route you cross the field above Northbrook Bridge, keeping the high garden walls to your left. Over a farm gate straight ahead, you join a footpath. In half-a-mile the grass pathway leads to concrete farm buildings and broadens into a cart track. Along this track you cross the line of the Roman Akeman Street, but your track continues straight on to reach Kirtlington in just under a mile.

At the edge of Kirtlington village the required track back to Tackley turns off to the right. However, it is worth wandering along the metalled road into Kirtlington village, with its lovely stone-built cottages, much of the building material having been taken from the Kirtlington quarries west of the village beside the Oxford canal.

Rejoin the track junction which you left at the village edge. Your track lies ahead, leaving the cart track you came on from Northbrook, to your right. This broad stone covered track descends towards the Cherwell. In half-a-mile a wood borders the right of the track. It hides the extensive workings of the stone quarries and the Oxford canal, upon which it had a wharf.

Another half-a-mile takes you down beside the canal at Pigeon Lock. Walk over the tail-end bridge. The footpath now becomes more difficult, but is quite well signposted. Over the gate and white bridge beside the lock, the path takes you to the far side of Flights Mill. The ford is just short of the weir which lets water down from the canal into the Cherwell, but to keep your feet dry, pass over the weir footbridge. The footpath now leads to the cement bridge which lies over a stream in the pasture in front of you. Once through the field gate beyond the bridge turn left on to a bridleway, and in 100 yards take the path to the right.

Half-a-mile of soft grass track brings you to the level crossing at Tackley Halt. Turn right and rejoin the village street at the **King's Arms.**

## 8½ mile walk

Follow the 4 mile walk to Northbrook Bridge. From Northbrook Bridge walk to the left hand corner of the field which you have crossed into and follow the gravel road into Northbrook. At the far end of the hamlet take a footpath leading behind a row of solitary cottages on the left of the road. The footpath curves round to the right and woodland comes into view along the left horizon. You come to a gate and a road. The path continues over them, and in 300 yards oak woods will border the left of the path for some 200 yards. At the end of the wood, turn right along a broad grass track. In half-a-mile on the left are Mushroom Cottages. Turn right at the cross path here, keeping the hedgerow to your left. Recross the metalled road and follow the lane ahead into Northbrook. Return to Tackley either by the route through Kirtlington which forms part of the 5½ mile walk or the route along the Oxford canal which is shorter and forms part of the 4 mile walk.

# Area 4

**Woodstock, Blenheim Park, Blenheim Palace**

**2 miles**

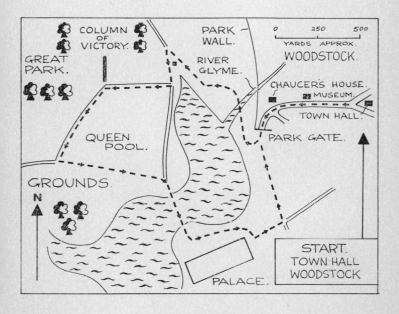

**How to get there:** By bus from Oxford or Banbury or by car using the A34 Oxford to Chipping Norton road.

**Refreshments:** There are numerous inns and cafes in Woodstock and a cafe at Blenheim Palace, open at certain times.

**What to see:** The historic town of Woodstock; the Oxford City and County Museum in Fletcher's House, a museum of rural life. Blenheim Park and the Palace.

The walk starts at the town hall in the centre of Woodstock. Set off towards the gate to Blenheim Park. On your right, in turn, are the City and County Museum and Chaucer's House. You turn a corner to your left and the gate is ahead. Walking into the Park turn sharp right along the side wall. There is a narrow metalled service road which runs gently downhill towards the lakeside which is on your left. It crosses the River Glyme which acts as an inflow to the lake by an ornamental bridge. The path then swings left, away from the Park wall and Woodstock. In about 300 yards you will come to a track junction at the tip of the lake with a cottage situated on your left. Take the left turn and a few yards past the cottage turn right up the slope, over which passes a footpath, to the Column of Victory which is situated about 400 yards away.

Blenheim Park and Gardens were laid out by Capability Brown who is supposed to have planned the trees and avenues to left and right of the Column to correspond with the troop formations at the Battle of Blenheim.

The Column shows the Duke of Marlborough dressed as a Roman and round the base of the memorial are records of his battles. From here an avenue runs directly to the north front of Blenheim Palace, a mile away in the distance. The footpath runs somewhat indistinctly down from the Column to the south west and meets another Park road which takes internal traffic to Park Farm. When you join this road, turn left on to it. It gradually descends to the Grand Bridge over the Lake.

The bridge is almost 400 feet long and the centre span exceeds 100 feet. On the bridge are rooms intended for use in the summer, and from the main span, fine views can be obtained over the lake and palace. Cross the bridge to the Palace front, turning left along it, the path then runs beside the car park and down the avenue of elms. Take the first turn left and leave the Park through the Palace Gate, returning to the Town Hall.

# Area 5

**Otmoor, Oddington, Charlton-on-Otmoor, Fencott**

**3½ and 4 miles**

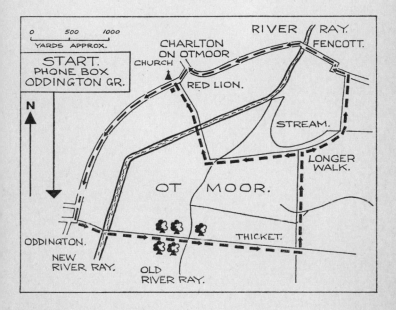

**How to get there:** By road using A43 Oxford to Bicester and turning off to Islip and Oddington.

**Refreshments: The Red Lion** at Charlton-on-Otmoor.

**What to see:** Otmoor, an area of extremely low-lying and unspoilt countryside. The enclosure of Otmoor led to riots in the surrounding villages. See the villages of Oddington, Fencott and Charlton-on-Otmoor and take a look inside Charlton church.

21

There are two precautions to be taken over these two walks. Firstly, even in high summer, there can be deep mud patches in the centre of Otmoor, so that suitable footwear is required, and secondly, part of the walk is within the danger area of the Otmoor Rifle Range, and, as the stop butts indicated by the warning notice are obscured by high hedgerows, you could wander through the area without realising it. So keep a look out for the red flags, and keep off the central path of Otmoor when they are flying.

Both walks begin and end at the telephone box on Oddington green. Pass over the rim of Otmoor by way of the bridle path which leaves the green; it soon crosses the sluggishly-flowing watercourse of the New River Ray. The track runs straight ahead, between elm trees, and almost due east. Within a mile you will cross the old course of the River Ray. Soon after the bridge the track narrows to a footpath. **Take care over the rifle range** which will appear to your right immediately before you enter a dense and damp thicket of hawthorne and bramble.

Emerging from the thicket, you will be close to the centre of Otmoor, where four radial footpaths meet. Turn left on to the line of a Roman road which linked Bicester to Roman building at Beckley on the southern side of the moor. This is, for the most part, now a wide bridle path, and you will soon cross a further deep, but slow moving, watercourse. Continue for under half-a-mile to the end of the track. At this point the two walks divide. For the $3\frac{1}{2}$ mile walk turn left and for the 4 mile walk, turn right.

Turning left, you follow another deep drainage ditch on your right. Enclosure of Otmoor made the paths and tracks take straight but angular courses. Leaving the drainage ditch which swings away to the right the track runs straight across the flat moor—at an even elevation of 60 feet. After the track has crossed a major drainage ditch, turn right and then cross the New River Ray. The track ascends sharply over the rim of Otmoor into Charlton-on-Otmoor. Turn left by the church and follow the metalled road for $\frac{3}{4}$ mile into Oddington, where the walk ends.

## 4 mile walk

From the junction noted in the $3\frac{1}{2}$ mile walk, turn right, keeping the deep drainage ditch to your left, shortly crossing it. The track swings gradually round to the left and rises up to the road in Fencott. Turn left through Fencott. You leave the settlement by crossing the River Ray. Follow the road into Charlton-on-Otmoor. Go straight through the village and on to Oddington, where the walk ends.

# Area 6

## East and West Hanney, Lyford, Charney Bassett, Denchworth
## 2½ and 6 miles

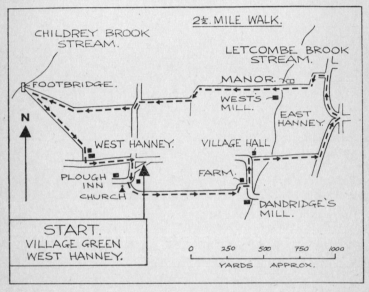

**How to get there:** The walks begin on West Hanney green. Use the Oxford bus service 300 between Wantage and Oxford. By car, turn off the A338 Wantage to Frilford road, at East Hanney.

**Refreshments:** The **Plough or Lamb** at West Hanney, the **Black Horse** at East Hanney, the **Fox** at Denchworth and the **Chequers** at Charney Bassett.

**What to see:** Villages typical of the Vale of the White Horse. Excellent collection of memorial brasses at West Hanney; Lyford Almshouses, founded in 1611; fine manor houses at

East Hanney, Denchworth and Lyford. The Manor at Charney Bassett and the Grange at Lyford.

## 2½ mile walk

For the short walk leave West Hanney green along the raised footway, running beneath the Old Rectory walls, to the church. Enter the churchyard and follow the path round the east of the building and through the churchyard. At the stile cross pasture. In 250 yards you will cross a bridle road which runs to Grove. In a further 200 yards you come to the back of Weirs Farm and the Mill House. Turn left and right through the farmyard, then left along the road for 50 yards. Turning right at the village hall, the asphalted footpath covers cobbles of the causeway which continues from West Hanney.

A metal bridge takes the path over the Letcombe Brook, Take the left fork after the bridge and turn left at the road. Walk through the village. In 300 yards, just past the post office, five roads meet. Take the first turning left and in a further 250 yards the first turning left again. This lane winds towards Philbeards Manor, which it skirts on the right. West's Mill lies a few yards to the left on the brook. You cross the stream by the bridge immediately in front of you, having passed the manor. The road degenerates into a bridle path running between elm trees, and emerges into fields with a sharp left turn. In 25 yards, along a footpath, take a sharp right turn along a field boundary. In a further 250 yards you join a road and turn left on the fringe of West Hanney. In 25 yards turn right over a plank bridge on a marked footpath. The path follows the hedgerow line straight ahead. In about ½ a mile you will come to the Childrey Brook with another plank bridge. This leads to Lyford, but for the short walk, turn your back on the bridge and walk straight ahead over the pasture to an obvious gate, then diagonally across the second pasture into which the gate leads. In the corner cross a stile and follow the lane on to the road where you turn left. The village green is in 100 yards.

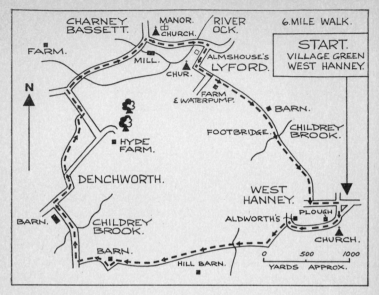

## 6 mile walk

Striking out from the green to the church, follow church street round to the right for 300 yards. Where it begins to turn sharply right take the bridle path to the left opposite Aldworths. Within a mile the path gently descends and ends on the road into Denchworth. Turn right into the village and at the junction there, turn right again. In 200 yards the road bends left and then right. At this point follow an indicated footpath. In ¾ mile turn left on to the road and follow it to Charney Bassett. Crossing the River Ock Bridge, turn right. Follow the road over the Ock and at the junction in 150 yards turn right. The Ayshcombe Almhouses are on the right, the church and manor are away to the right at the next junction, where you turn left.

Continue straight ahead up a farm track where the road turns left, in 100 yards. The track becomes a footpath and leads to the plank bridge over the Childrey Brook. Strike across the pasture ahead and follow the instructions in the short walk, which follows the same route back.

26

# Area 7

**Fyfield, Netherton, Hart's Weir, Northmoor, Bablockhythe, Northmoor Lock, Fyfield**

### 3, 6½ or 8 miles

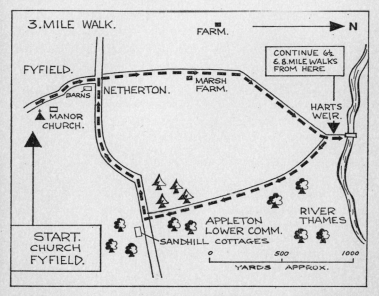

**How to get there:** Bristol/Oxford Omnibus services 466 and 467 from Swindon, Faringdon or Oxford. By car, using A420 Oxford to Faringdon road.

**Refreshments: The White Hart,** Fyfield, and the **Dun Cow** or **Red Lion** at Northmoor. Northmoor Lock serves sweets and ice cream during the summer.

**What to see:** Fyfield church and manor, the White Hart, Northmoor church, Rectory Farm, and a typically unspoiled English village, Characteristic scenery along the Upper Thames.

27

### 3 mile walk

You start from Fyfield church and take the road running north by the manor wall. It winds gradually downhill into the adjacent hamlet of Netherton. Beyond Netherton you reach a T-road junction. Go straight ahead along a bridle track slightly uphill and passing Marsh Farm, an old enclosure farm, on the right.

In some 200 yards the track narrows to a path. You are now on the top of the Corallian Limestone escarpment with the whole of the Upper Thames valley spread out in front of you. The path winds down the escarpment, initially between mature trees, then over fields to Hart's Weir on the Thames. The outline of the weir, backwater and cottage garden can be traced on the south bank of the river. Close by is a high arched wooden footbridge built by the Thames Conservancy which crosses the river, but for this short walk you spurn the bridge and retrace your footsteps from the riverside to the edge of the old garden, which you cross, bearing slightly left to meet the side of Appleton Lower Common Wood, beside which runs a footpath up the escarpment. Having crossed two stiles you will be joined by a coniferous plantation on your right and the footway now becomes a shaded path passing through deep woodland for 300 yards until you join the road near Sandhill Cottages. Turn right and follow this winding road for $\frac{3}{4}$ mile. You will regain the T-junction north of Fyfield. Turn left and retrace your footsteps to Fyfield church.

### 8 mile walk

Follow the 3 mile walk to Hart's Weir and cross the wooden Thames Conservancy footbridge there. The footpath across the meadows bears half right from the river bank. It is slightly difficult to trace across the field, but as one gets closer to the opposite hedge, the gap through which the footpath passes becomes obvious. Follow a cart track now running due north. A clear footpath takes over, following the edge of the field. Stiles and footbridges cross two deep streams bordering the fields. At the second footbridge you

28

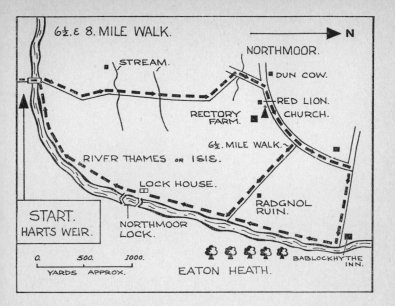

NORTHMOOR.

STREAM.

■ DUN COW.

RED LION.

RECTORY FARM.

▲ CHURCH.

6½. MILE WALK.

RIVER THAMES OR ISIS.

LOCK HOUSE.

RADGNOL RUIN.

START. HARTS WEIR.

NORTHMOOR LOCK.

0    500.    1000.

YARDS  APPROX.

EATON  HEATH.

BABLOCKHYTHE INN.

change position from the left hand side of the hedge to the right hand side. At this point the outbuildings of Northmoor come into sight. Passing round the side of the meadow, you take the first gate on the left and turning left, walk to the Newbridge-Northmoor road. Turn right on to this quiet lane, little used by traffic, and follow it for 200 yards, turning right again at the junction into Northmoor village. The **Dun Cow** is behind you and the **Red Lion** ahead. Passing this inn, you come to the unspoiled church on the right, with Rectory Farm, its unique dovecote and granary, standing south of the church.

From Northmoor church you follow the road for a mile passing isolated farms and houses to left and right. Just beyond Lower Farm you turn right along a private road which runs beside a caravan park to the river bank at the site of the Bablockhythe ferry. At the ferry turn right along the River Thames towpath.

The path is quite clear for its entire length to the Hart's Weir footbridge. You pass through pastures which help form some of the best river scenery on the Isis. On the opposite bank Eaton Heath rises steeply.

A mile and a half from Bablockhythe you come to Northmoor Lock, quite isolated in the fields. It is worth bearing in mind that 'Beware of the Bull' signs ought to be heeded, although you usually find that a bull grazing with cattle is quite docile.

From Northmoor Lock it is a further mile along the towpath to the footbridge which we need. Crossing the footbridge, you may either retrace your footsteps to Marsh Farm and Fyfield, or take the continuation of the 3 mile walk up the side of Appleton Lower Common Wood.

## 6½ mile walk

Follow the 8 mile walk to Northmoor church, and 450 yards from the church just short of Pencots Farm, which is on the left, take the turning off the road, to the right. The track passes over fields to the ruin of Radgnoll Farm and continues straight ahead to join the towpath about 400 yards below Northmoor Lock. When you reach the towpath, turn right towards Northmoor Lock, and continue along the route given for the 8 mile walk.

# Area 8

**Abingdon, Andersey Island, Swift Ditch, Culham and Sutton Courtenay**

**2, 2½ and 5 miles**

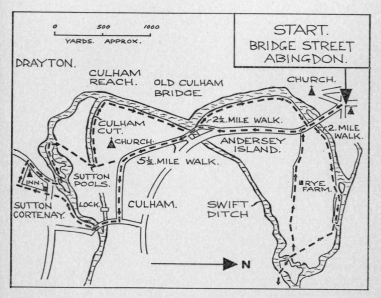

**How to get there:** Oxford Omnibus service from Oxford, Wantage or Didcot, or by car using the A34 from Oxford or Newbury or the A415 from Faringdon or Wallingford. You may reach Abingdon by rail to Radley, thence to Abingdon by bus.

**Refreshments:** Of the numerous inns try the **Crown and Thistle** or **Punchbowl** in Abingdon, or the **George and Dragon** or **Fish** at Sutton Courtenay. Trotman's cafe in Ock Street, Abingdon, serves a good bun and coffee.

**What to see:** At Abingdon, the Abbey buildings; St. Helen's church and St. Nicolas' church; the domestic architecture in East St. Helen Street; the County Hall and the Old Gaol. There are medieval bridges at Abingdon and Culham. See Culham House and Manor. The church, and abundant domestic architecture at Sutton Courtenay is well worth close examination.

Abingdon was the county town of Berkshire until 1869, consequently many public buildings echo past glories. The fine County Hall built by Christopher Kempster in 1682, looks on to the market place. St. Nicholas' church, originally for the lay people associated with the Abbey, adjoins the Abbey gateway and links with the former municipal buildings and the old Grammar School.


## 2 mile walk

Take a look inside the Roysse Room in Bridge Street. John Roysse, mercer of London, re-founded the Grammar School here in 1563. As a typical Elizabethan conceit it measures 63 feet in length, was intended for 63 pupils and was built in Roysse's 63rd year. The school moved to the Park in 1870.

From the Roysse Room, the walk takes you down Bridge Street. You pass the **Crown and Thistle,** an old coaching inn, on the left, with the County Police Station of 1857 and the County Goal of 1811 (on the right), the latter, variously called the Bastille of Berkshire.

Abingdon Bridge, called Burford Bridge by some and standing as a corruption of Boroughford, which it replaced, is worth examining. Largely reconstructed in 1927, the sole original medieval portion is on the Abingdon side. The bridge was substantially widened in the 19th century and underneath one can see the junction of medieval and modern stonework.

Continue from the bridge along the causeway, which crosses Andersey Island. Built by the Guild of the Holy Cross, a merchant guild in the town, it gave a dry route in time of flood.

Half a mile along the Causeway, which is followed by the line of the turnpike of 1733, you come to the first milestone from Abingdon (although it is misplaced in terms of distance from the market place). Here follow the Causeway which branches through trees to the right and crosses Swift Ditch, now a backwater but once the original course of the Thames. The old Culham Bridge, like Abingdon Bridge, is medieval on one side and late 18th century on the other, where it was widened.

Follow the towing path alongside the river back to Abingdon. On the opposite bank you will see the cast iron bridge over the River Ock at its confluence with the Thames. The inscription *erected by the Wilts & Berks Canal Company AD 1824 cast at Acramans Bristol* may just be visible. Re-enter Abingdon along Bridge Street.

### 5½ mile walk

Follow the 2 mile walk to Culham Bridge and from there continue past the toll house at the eastern end of the bridge. Turn right and follow the road into Culham. There is a good footpath alongside the road. Culham House lies behind high walls to the left and the Elizabethan manor and dovecote is opposite the church, which is situated over the green to the right. Follow the road round to the left. At the junction in 200 yards, turn right. On the left, beside the Thames, is the site of Culham Brick Works, with the extensive clay pit deeply cut into the hill side at the far end of the site.

Cross Sutton Courtenay Bridge and follow the footpath half right which runs across the meadows beside the Thames. It enters Sutton Courtenay opposite the **Fish Inn.** Walk up the lane on the left of the inn and turn right through the churchyard and notice the 13th century chancel. The choir stalls have three misericords. In the graveyard is the tomb of a former Prime Minister, the Earl of Oxford and Asquith.

At the western end of the churchyard turn right along the edge of the green, passing the **George and Dragon Inn.** At the Wharf, a large house on the left opposite where the road turns sharply right, you turn left up a narrow footpath which crosses Sutton Pools, a series of weirs and plunge pools. Over the last weir, bear right along the footpath across meadows to the high wooden bridge spanning Culham Cut. Cross the bridge. Here you may either turn left and follow the tow path back to Abingdon or go straight ahead through Culham re-tracing your footsteps to Culham Bridge then following the tow path back to Abingdon as indicated in the 2½ mile walk.

**2 mile walk**

Cross the main span of Abingdon Bridge and take the steps down to the left which descend to the tow path. Follow the tow path to the right as far as Abingdon Lock. Pass through the Lock grounds continuing along the tow path. Go through the grey Thames Conservancy gate into Ferry Boat Field. Follow the path across it to the bridge which takes you over the Thames backwater. Further on, a narrow footbridge will take you over the Swift Ditch, the original course of the river, and you will have crossed the lock chamber on this course of the stream.

At Swift Ditch retrace your steps across the two bridges to Ferry Boat Field. The path lies half-left from the second bridge and extends for 200 yards over the meadow to a gate. Beyond the gate the footpath very quickly becomes a track and passing Rye Farm to the right, rejoins the main road at the end of Abingdon Bridge. Turn right to cross the bridge. The walk ends at Abingdon market place.

# Area 9

**Wittenham Clumps, Little Wittenham, Sinodun Hills and Dorchester, Day's Lock**

**1, 1¾, 3½ and 4 miles**

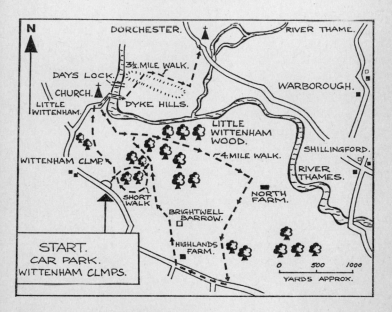

**How to get there:** The best way is by car to the park just below Wittenham Clumps on the Little Wittenham to Brightwell road.

**Refreshments:** There is no inn at Little Wittenham, although it has a small shop. Among the several inns at Dorchester are the **George** and the **Chequers.**

**What to see:** Wittenham Clumps and Camp; Little Wittenham village; Dorchester Abbey; Day's Lock, and the all-round panoramas over the Thames and Downs from the Sinodun Hills.

The walks begin at the car park below Wittenham Clumps.

## The 1 mile walk

For this walk it is merely a question of following the footpath from the car park to the hill camp on the right hand hill of the Wittenham pair. To walk round the camp, from which good views may be had over the varied surroundings, and back to the park is just under a mile and may be linked with a walk to the left hand clump also. Look carefully at the Beech trees. One has some 20 lines of verse carved on the bark in praise of the surrounding countryside.

## The 1¾ mile walk

Ascend to Wittenham Clump, the left hand one, and walk over the summit. From here the footpath leads downhill to Little Wittenham and joins the road by the church. Keep the church tower as a point of reference, and when you get there, examine it closely and you will see that its windows reflect the four suits in a card pack. They are shaped like a heart, diamond, spade and club, built it is said, by a reformed card player!

You may return either the same way, or by taking the lower path which leads into Little Wittenham Woods. If you take this latter course, on reaching the edge of the woodland, follow the path for some 250 yards then bear right. You will come to a stile, cross it into a broad ride, turning left along it. At the end of the ride cross a further stile and turn right alongside the wood through which you have passed. This footpath leads directly up the northern side of Wittenham Camp, and from the summit it is an easy walk to the car park. It is very important to keep to the public rights of way in Wittenham Wood and the neighbourhood; gamekeepers patrol the area.

## 3½ mile walk extension

Follow the 1¾ mile walk to Little Wittenham church and continue along the road to Day's Lock crossing to the opposite bank of the Thames, from which one of the best views of Wittenham Clumps may be had.

Take the footpath to Dorchester which bears left from the Lock and passes through a gap in the Dyke Hills, a very early set of earthen embankments. On the far side of the hills the path turns right along the earthwork which ends as the path broadens into a track, which turning left, leads quickly through Bridge End into Dorchester.

Take a look at the fine domestic architecture in this village. An important stopping place is the splendid Abbey church and its associated museum.

It is best to return to Little Wittenham by retracing your footsteps by way of the Dyke Hills to Day's Lock. At the church decide whether to go to the car park directly or to take the alternative route indicated in the second part of the 1¾ mile walk through Little Wittenham Wood. Either way, it is a pleasant afternoon's ramble.


## 4 mile walk

You begin the walk by ascending Wittenham Clump, leaving the site by a footpath from the NE corner of the earthwork. You descend, with a small wood on your left. A stile leads into a long and wide ride to your left through the woods. Having turned into this ride walk along it for some 200 yards, cross the stile on your right and take the footpath into Little Wittenham Woods. In a further 200 yards this footpath joins a second but narrower ride. Turn sharply right on to it and continue along it to the eastern edge of Wittenham Wood.

Beech and Oak wood, with conifers interspersed, constitute a woodland profuse with wildlife. The gamekeepers hereabouts act keenly to keep walkers to the legal footpaths.

You leave the woodland suddenly. Continue ahead by a

path along the field boundary for 400 yards. At the ruin of Lowerhill Farm, on the left, the path becomes a track which you follow for some 500 yards. Shortly before the prominent buildings of North Farm, the track is crossed at right angles by the line of a Roman road. Turn right along it over the gentle ridge of the Sinodun Hills. In $\frac{3}{4}$ mile from the summit the path joins a new road round Brightwell-cum-Sotwell. Turn right along the verge and at Highlands Farm turn obliquely right over the stile striking along the path towards Brightwell Barrow. The footpath from the barrow back to Wittenham Camp is not too clear and runs virtually directly across country, but the eminence of Wittenham Clump is always obvious as a directional reference point. From the Clump return to the car park.

# Area 10

**Letcombe Regis, Letcombe Bassett, the Ridgeway and Lambourn Downs — 3½, 7 and 15 miles**

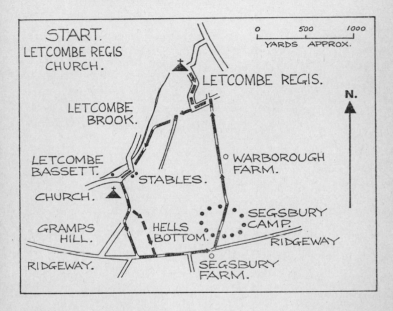

**How to get there:** By car through Wantage. The walks begin at Letcombe Regis.

**Refreshments: The Sparrow or Greyhound** at Letcombe Regis and the **Yew Tree** at Letcombe Bassett.

**What to see:** The ancient churches at Letcombe Bassett and Letcombe Regis, fine examples of domestic architecture in both villages, and some of the best downland countryside in southern England.

A small portion of these walks lie in Berkshire. Before the local authority boundary changed, the whole area was in the Royal county, but the bulk has now been transferred to Oxfordshire. They cover some of the best countryside along the chalk downland and frequently command extensive views over the Vale of the White Horse, and southwards towards Newbury and the Hampshire Downs.

### 3½ mile walk

From Letcombe Regis church, take the road running south which leads to the downs. It winds slightly uphill and has a raised footpath on the left and a series of ancient cottages adjacent.

The road turns sharply right, then left and left again. At the second left turn, as it issues into open country, take the indicated footpath to the right. It runs between mature trees as a bridlepath for some 300 yards, giving glimpses of the chalk escarpment a mile to the left across the chalk bench. The route turns left and in a hundred yards a narrow footpath branches to the right and runs slightly downhill towards the deeply incised valley of the upper Letcombe brook.

The footpath can easily be traced and follows the line of the brook, passing upstream, along the top of a steeply sloping pasture. You will pass an old mill on your right and several cottages on the opposite side of the valley. In about ¾ mile Letcombe Bassett comes into view. Descending to the road at White's Farm, turn right, and passing racehorse stables on your left, go to the road junction at the village centre.

Down to your right, behind the houses, is the site of the famous watercress beds, while a little further along the road to the right is Arabella's Cottage, almost toppling into the water. This is the house mentioned in Thomas Hardy's novel 'Jude the Obscure' where Jude passing from Lambourn (Marygreen) through Letcombe (Cresscombe) to Oxford (Christminster) came across Arabella washing pig's chitterlings — but Arabella was the beginning of poor Jude's downfall!

At the road junction turn left and walk uphill. On the right lies the church of St Michael looking up the impressive hollow into the chalk, called the Devil's Punchbowl.

On your left at the edge of the settlement is the Old Rectory. It was here that Dean Swift, author of Gulliver's Travels, lived for some years. Above the house a lengthy barn is of early cruck construction, and in one place giant beams, hewn from whole oak trees, reach from floor level to the apex of the roof. Local tradition maintains that various timbers came from some of Bristol's Merchantmen.

The road from Letcombe begins to run steeply uphill and is cut into the chalk hillside and enclosed in vegetation. In 200 yards it bears right. An interesting exposure of the middle chalk lies to the right — probably the remains of a chalkpit which provided road mending and building material for the village in the early 19th century.

Opposite the chalkpit, a footpath leads from the left of the road and gradually passes downhill into a small valley called Hell's Bottom. Passing through a woodland in the bottom, you bear right and begin climbing steeply on the side of the chalk escarpment to reach the Ridgeway, half-a-mile above.

As an alternative route, should the season be such that a thick layer of mud covers the ploughed land along this footpath, or growing crops mask the way, you may continue up the road. In 200 yards a branch forks left. Take this route to Parsonage Hill and in 600 yards you will reach the summit of the downland on the Ridgeway, slightly west of the footpath's exit from Hell's Bottom.

Turn left along the Ridgeway. You are now passing down one of the most useful and ancient routes in England, used equally in mediaeval times and during the 18th and 19th centuries to give a dry cross-country route. Although called the Ridgeway, you will probably note that it is set back slightly from the edge of the crest so that it is not always possible to gain the widest views over the Vale of the White Horse.

Follow the undulations of the Ridgeway for half-a-mile. Opposite Segsbury Farm, a green road leads left and neatly bisects the ramparts of Segsbury Camp. If you want more fresh air and a good view, divert your path round the top of the rampart, rejoining the green road on the north side of the camp. At this point the road plunges over the chalk into Letcombe Regis at the hill foot.

### The 7 and 15 mile walks

Follow the 3½ mile walk to the point beyond Letcombe Bassett where the roads divided, and we turn off to Parsonage Hill. At this point, ignore the route to the left and continue straight up to the Ridgeway at Gramp's Hill. Turn right along the ancient route and follow it. You will have some splendid views across the Vale, and in some places, into the distance towards Swindon.

In a mile you pass the distinctively placed small clump of conifers on the left, called Folly Clump, and correctly so, for it can be seen for miles around. Soon, racehorse gallops will border the route on your left, while over to the right you will be able to look into the extensive and impressive gully called the Devil's Punchbowl, with Hackpen Hill beyond it.

Follow the Ridgeway from Folly Clump for a further mile. At the Wantage to Lambourn road, close to the Sparsholt Firs radio mast, turn left along the metalled road for several hundred yards, until you reach a rough farm track bearing left. It is partly the entrance road to Greendown Farm, but also leads deeply into the Lambourn Downs. Follow the track for two miles, passing Greendown Farm away to the left, until you come to Sheepdrove Farm. There are barns on the right and a farm cottage on the left backed by a small beech wood; the place-name indicated earlier agricultural importance. In a further 700 yards is an isolated dutch barn near Stancombe Down where several tracks across the downland meet.

Take the track to your left, having turned through almost 90 degrees. In roughly 400 yards of largely downhill walking the metalled road turns right and continues as the 15 mile walk.

At this point, if you wish to use the 7 mile walk, ignore

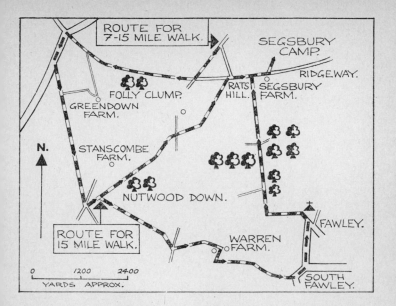

the hard road and carry straight ahead along a well-defined bridleway for just over a mile, gradually climbing up the dip slope of the chalk. Having ascended Nutwood Down, you will come to a junction of tracks, at which point you have the choice of turning left, to cross the Ridgeway in less than a mile and descending Gramp's Hill into Letcombe Bassett, returning to Letcombe Regis in the reverse direction along the footpath you used earlier.

Alternatively, you might choose to walk straight ahead, in which case you will join the Ridgeway at Rat's Hill, near the summit of Parsonage Hill. Turn right along the Ridgeway for about 700 yards as far as the green road opposite Segsbury Farm. Here turn left through Segsbury Camp and follow the concluding route of the 3½ mile walk.

### Continuation of 15 mile walk

For the full 15 miles, from Stancombe Down, turn right at the point where the 7 mile walk went ahead. Follow the

43

metalled road down the dry valley into Eastbury Bottom. From here the road ascends quite steeply up the side of Warren Down, and from the summit runs gently downhill to farm cottages belonging to Warren Farm. Continue to Warren Farm, turning sharply right through the farmyard, you continue for 300 yards, then turn sharply left, walking with a lengthy woodland immediately on your right. You will find the walk quite easy, as it descends gradually down another dry valley into South Fawley.

In the village take the public road ahead; in 150 yards bear left at the junction and head into North Fawley which is about $\frac{3}{4}$ mile away on the skyline. Turn left up the village street, passing the church on the right. It is a good example of a small village church designed in entirety by George Street, who began his notable architectural career at Wantage.

Some 700 yards from the church the track turns sharply right. As a wide cart track it leads to the Ridgeway within three miles. You will quickly pass barns on your left. The track is now bordered on the right by a long plantation. The small collection of houses and barns at Letcombe Bowers is just visible through the trees on the right, while to your left are wide views over another of the countless dry valleys in this area. The track gradually climbs the back of the chalk dip slope as a ridge between two dry valleys, and a mile from Letcombe Bowers joins the Ridgeway.

Turn right along the Ridgeway, and in 300 yards you will be at Segsbury Farm. Turn left through Segsbury Camp, and follow the route which concludes the $3\frac{1}{2}$ mile walk.

# Area 11

**Ewelme, Down Farm, Sliding Hill, Britwell Park**

**3, 3½ or 5½ miles**

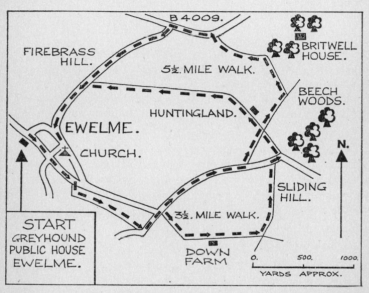

**How to get there:** By road using A423 to Benson or B480 to Watlington. The B4009 linking Benson and Watlington passes through Ewelme. All walks begin at the **Greyhound Inn,** Ewelme.

**Refreshments: The Greyhound Inn,** Ewelme, or the **Red Lion** at Britwell Salome.

**What to see:** Historic Almshouses, church and school at Ewelme, built by Alice, Duchess of Suffolk in the 15th century. Ewelme watercress beds, Britwell House, Park and Monument.

## The 3 mile walk

With Ewelme's **Greyhound Inn** on your right walk east through the village. The church and school will be high above you to the left. In a few yards the main road turns right and ascends Rabbit Hill, but ignore this route and carry straight ahead out of the village. On the right in about 200 yards, behind Common Cottage is Cow Common with its village cricket square in the centre. Bear right and follow the path over the outfield to the stile which crosses the boundary fence.

The path follows a shallow bottom to an elongated saucer of a dry valley for about $\frac{3}{4}$ mile over close cropped pasture. At the end of the field you pass through the hedgerow using a stile and on to the road. Turn left for about 150 yards to the road junction (the $3\frac{1}{2}$ mile walk leaves the route here) and carry straight on.

The road curves gradually round to the right and passes imperceptibly uphill, between barley fields and low hawthorn hedgerows. Away to your right are views to the edge of the Chiltern Hills on Swyncombe Down and Sliding Hill.

In $\frac{3}{4}$ mile leave the public road by taking a wide bridle path to the left; 400 yards along the track you will come to a crossing of bridle roads.

Taking the farm road to your left you will come, in 200 yards, to the brick and metal barns at Huntingland, widely visible in these parts. Continue uphill along the track for about 400 yards. The route gradually turns to the left, the gradient will flatten and the track begin to descend gently, offering splendid views over the Thames valley to the Berkshire Downs, Wittenham Clumps, Didcot and Wallingford.

Almost a mile beyond Huntingland the bridle track joins the B4009. Bear left on to the road and descend Firebrass Hill into Ewelme. Passing small housing estates to your left and right on the outskirts of the village, bear left to the church and walk down through the church yard to the Greyhound Inn.

## The 3½ mile walk

Follow the 3 mile walk to the end of Cow Common to the point indicated in the text, where the 3½ mile walk branches off.

At the T-road junction, a footpath turns right from the road, passing uphill. There is a hedgerow on your right. Walking over a brow pass through a gate, with a long copse to your left, and follow the field boundary round to your right.

You will quickly descend to a metalled farm road. The footpath actually winds behind Down Farm to the left, although this road does lead straight through the farm yard. Walk some 350 yards beyond Downs Farm along the metalled road which runs in a fine avenue. A track joins the road from the right. Immediately to the left a footpath follows the fence — the first fence beyond Downs Farm on this side. Take this route, and walk gradually uphill. A mature hedgerow will eventually join the path from the right. Keep the hedge to your right and descend over a pasture to the road near the foot of Sliding Hill.

Turn right along the road for a few yards. At the cross roads, with beech woods to your right turn left (5½ mile walk branches off here) to the barns of Huntingland, then follow the 3 mile walk to its conclusion at Ewelme.

## The 5½ mile walk

Follow the 3½ mile walk to the point indicated in the text where the 5½ mile walk branches off. At the turning towards Huntingland take care. The bridle path towards the barns is followed for a few yards, but at a crossing of tracks take the right hand turn which leads towards Britwell Salome. It runs along a broad pebble-covered farm road. In 400 yards you will come to a deep hedgerow on your left. It conceals a footpath. Follow the path keeping Britwell House and Park to your right.

The path gradually descends, then rises and bears left. In about 550 yards you will join the B4009. Turn left on to the road and follow it to the next junction in about 400 yards. At this point turn left and follow the road into Ewelme, gradually descending Firebrass Hill. Enter the village using the conclusion of the 3 mile walk.

# Area 12

**Steventon, Wood's Farm, West Hendred, East Hendred**

**5¼ miles**

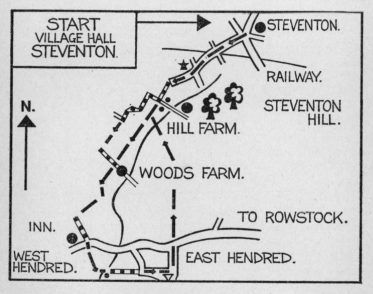

**How to get there:** By road using the A34 to Steventon or by bus from Oxford, Abingdon or Newbury.

**Refreshments:** The **Hare** at West Hendred or the **Plough** and **Eyston Arms** at East Hendred.

The walk begins at the village hall on the southern end of Steventon green, where you may quite easily park. Cross the A34 with care to the War Memorial and walk along the Causeway. On your left you will see a series of substantial houses of architectural distinction. There are some fine and varied facades which improve in quantity and quality as you approach the church at the far end of the Causeway.

In some 400 yards along the Causeway take a rapid right and then left turn by the school and continue along the second half of the Causeway. Beyond the level crossing are several fine examples of domestic architecture, mostly of timber-frame construction. The Priory, near the church of St. Michael, has wings dating from the 15th and 16th centuries, while the solar wing is late 14th century.

At the church, the raised, stone-covered, Causeway ends. In the opposite direction it can be traced as far as Milton and in medieval times provided a dry route for the monks from the Steventon Priory, which then belonged to a cell of the Abbey of Bec.

Passing the church to your right follow the metalled road for 500 yards to Hill Farm. Here you may slightly shorten the route of this walk by following the footpath straight ahead which will take you directly to Wood's Farm, but in poor weather this is a wet route. It is better, perhaps, to take the bridle path to Wood's Farm.

At Hill Farm turn right along a track beside barns. In 200 yards, near the electricity cables, the track turns left through ninety degrees and in almost half a mile the track turns right. At this point carry straight on along a footpath which will take you beside a field boundary on the right, then through a gate and over an open field to a pair of cottages which are clearly visible from some distance away.

At Wood's Farm Cottages turn left on to a track to the orchard before Wood's Farm. A footpath is indicated by handingposts and it is here that the shorter footpath from Hill Farm joins the main route. Turn right along the footpath. It passes beside the orchard on the left which tumbles down to the incised course of the Ginge Brook. Keep the brook to your left for a few hundred yards. When it turns sharply away from you to the left keep straight ahead over an open field. At this point the footpath is not well defined and you will have to aim across the field to the far hedge at a point where the hedge zig-zags away from you. For a long distance sight-line keep the white clapper boarding of the Hare Inn at West Hendred on the skyline. That is the direction you need to aim for.

When you reach the far hedgerow you will find a narrow track in a cutting leading straight ahead. Follow it until you emerge from the cutting in two hundred yards and take the well-defined track to your left which turns south to the main Wantage-Rowstock road, which you will cross in 500 yards.

Should you perhaps feel thirsty, you will find the Hare Inn a short distance to your right along the road, but should you wish to continue the walk, carefully cross the road, which is here quite deeply entrenched. The footpath continues across fields from the opposite side of the road. You will follow a field boundary for 400 yards. When you come to the thatched cottage on the right, turn left keeping the hedgerow on your right.

At the end of the field, you cross a stile, and take the reasonably well-worn footpath down to the Ginge Brook which you cross using a stout wooden footbridge. Here the path divides. Take the left branch to East Hendred Mill, the wooden front of which lies a hundred yards across the field. A gate and bridge will take you on to a road which rises into East Hendred village.

In almost 500 yards you will come to a cross roads. Walk straight over, passing the Plough Inn on your right. In a hundred yards you may bear right into the centre of the village, or continue straight on to the White Road, where the walk continues by turning left to the main Wantage to Rowstock road. The footpath you need is straight across the main road, just to the left of the junction, where a well indicated track leads off from the road.

Follow the track for some 400 yards, passing sheds on your right. Cross the gate beyond the sheds and walk straight on, almost due north, following the track downhill for about 700 yards. It will give you a good view over broken countryside into the claylands of the Vale of the White Horse. When you have reached this point the track narrows to a footpath following a field boundary running parallel with a series of overhead electricity wires and pylons to the right.

The path enters a small copse and in a yard or so crosses the Ginge Brook by a footbridge. Turn right and follow the line of the brook, passing under the overhead wires. From this point Hill Farm lies quite clearly ahead in some 300 yards. The footpath takes you between the farm buildings and you rejoin the metalled road which goes ahead to Steventon church.

Retrace your steps along the Causeway, and the walk ends at Steventon village hall.

# Area 13

**East Hendred, Ridgeway, Land's End, East Ginge, West Hendred and Old Street**

**5½, 8½ and 10 miles**

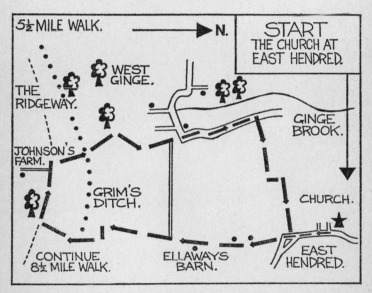

**How to get there:** By road or bus to East Hendred using the A417 from Wantage or Rowstock. The walks begin at East Hendred church.

**Refreshments:** The **Eyston Arms** or the **Plough** at East Hendred or the **Blue Boar** at North Heath on the Old Street walk.

**What to see:** The pretty village of East Hendred, Champ's chapel, the 13th century church of St Augustine and the manor houses at Hendred. An immense amount of Downland scenery.

# The 5½ mile walk

The walk begins in the centre of East Hendred at the church. Take the road which runs south from the village. At first it gently rises on to the lower chalk above the village. In 800 yards you will clear the settlement and the straight road will lead ahead towards the escarpment of the Berkshire Downs. Pass isolated barns to your right and left, called Parsonage Barn (with intricate brick patterns) and Ellaway's Barn. On your left lies the expanse of the nuclear laboratories at Harwell, here partly hidden behind the ornamental parkland that was once the site of Down's House. For some 800 yards from Down's House the road enters an avenue and turns sharply left then right and begins to ascend to the Ridgeway very steeply. (Continuation for the 8½ and 10 mile walks from here).

From the summit are excellent views in virtually every direction. The walk continues by turning right and following the ancient Ridgeway. On your left for 200 yards runs woodland, with Cuckhamsley Hill to the right. At the end of the woodland and on the opposite side of the Ridgeway you pass a prominent triangulation station. From this point, in 400 yards, the track to Johnson's Farm leaves the Ridgeway to the left. A few yards further on is a single pedestrian gate leaving the Ridgeway to the right (for conclusion of the 8½ mile walk follow on from here). Go through the gate and follow the footpath over the brow of the scarp, keeping the field fence to your left. Very soon you pass through a field gate and the pathway becomes a track which winds down the escarpment between ornamental woodland and small chalk quarries. This track is called White Way, and having levelled out at the foot of the hill passes through another gate adjacent to woodland on the left. The track now bears right across the field in front of you and emerges on the metalled road in the hamlet of East Ginge.

Keep straight on along the road, which on the left is tree lined. Walk for just over half a mile to where the trees degenerate to low hedgerow. Across the road passes the track called the Icknield Way. Turn right on to the track, which passes between ploughed fields. On your left a few hundred yards away are the obvious rises of Goldbury Hill and Park Hill. The track varies in quality and width. You should keep walking ahead, although the right of way actually does a sharp left and right turn, but a newish farm track through low conifers will take you on to the road between East Hendred to the Ridgeway, at the edge of the village.

Turn left. The road descends between trees into East Hendred and the church is some 800 yards away.

### The 8½ mile walk

Follow the 5½ mile walk as far as the Ridgeway. When you reach the summit, instead of turning right, carry straight on keeping the trees of the small coppice on your right. The grass track is quite clearly defined and it is bordered by race-horse gallops on the left. In half a mile the track bears gently right and soon begins to descend over Kilman Knoll Down. In a further three-quarters of a mile of descent you will join the East Ilsley to Farnborough road. Turn right along it and in 400 yards on the right will appear an isolated house. This is called Land's End, and what more appropriate name for such a distant and isolated spot? (10 mile walk continues from here).

In front of the house a track turns right off the road, then winds round to the left. This is the route back to the Ridgeway. In a hundred yards or so the track forks. Be careful to take the pebble covered right fork, which ascends and will soon take you through a beechwood on West Ginge Down.

Emerging from the wood, the track rises gently. It passes an isolated keeper's cottage and Lew's Barn, both of which back on to deep woodland on the left. Leaving the woodland behind, the track again rises gently and in 300 yards passes through a gate to join the Ridgeway. Turn right along the Ridgeway. On the right you pass the farm road down to Ridgeway Barn, and in about 400 yards, just a step or too short of the road down to the right leading to

55

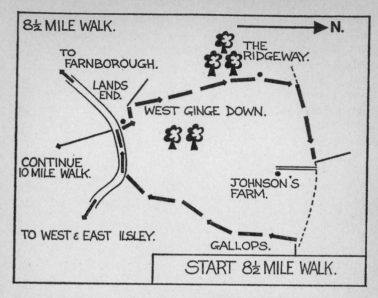

8½ MILE WALK. ——————→ N.

TO FARNBOROUGH.

THE RIDGEWAY.

LANDS END.

WEST GINGE DOWN.

CONTINUE 10 MILE WALK.

JOHNSON'S FARM.

TO WEST & EAST ILSLEY.

GALLOPS.

START 8½ MILE WALK.

Johnson's Farm, you will find a single pedestrian gate leading from the Ridgeway to the left. Take this footpath which leads down the escarpment to East Ginge and East Hendred. For details of the route follow the 5½ mile walk from the point indicated for the conclusion of the 8½ mile walk.

**The 10 mile walk**

This walk forms the only straight walk in this book. It begins in Oxfordshire, at East Hendred church, but ends in Berkshire, some ten miles away, at the Blue Boar Inn on the Wantage to Newbury road (B4494) at North Heath. Alternatively, you may shorten the walk by beginning at the Ridgeway above East Hendred (where you can park easily), or at Land's End. In both cases you will have to return by the reverse route, or arrange for someone to meet you.

The walk follows the line of Old Street, one of the ancient routes and Drove Roads crossing the Downland. It was much used when East Hendred had a market and was important in the wool trade of England, but now it is little used except by the discriminating walker who may want to get away from it all, for this walk studiously avoids the villages and hamlets of the Downs.

Leave East Hendred using the 5½ mile route to the Ridgeway, then follow the 8½ mile route as far as Land's End. At the isolated house at Land's End a track leaves the metalled road to the left and quickly ascends the side of Old Down. On Hernehill Down the track begins to level out and enters a strip of mixed woodland which encloses the track for some half a mile. Old Street emerges from the wood very suddenly on to the West Ilsley to Catmore road, which the walk follows for 300 yards.

The road bears right, but at this point the walk continues ahead across a field for 600 yards, and using a stile enters the side of Knapp's Copse. The route of Old Street is entirely well-defined and it again passes through a long woodland tunnel for almost a mile. Another track merges with the walk from the left at this point, and the walk continues for half a mile when it crosses the minor Stanmore to Peasemore road making a meeting point of five routes.

Cross the road and carry straight on. It is good, easy walking here, as Old Street runs gently down the dip slope of the chalk downland. Just over a mile from the five-way junction, a small track joins the walk from the left, and in 400 yards ahead the walk joins a metalled minor road. Turn left along it for a very short distance. It will take you round an isolated cottage on the right of the road, and beside the cottage garden, the track will leave the metalled road to the right.

Once again the walk is straight and clear and follows an undulating course for about a mile and a quarter to Hazelhanger Farm, which lies just to the right of the track.

You might get your feet wet crossing the ford at this point, but it makes for further variety along the line of this walk. The countryside has changed over the last mile or so, for the walk now crosses pebble beds and the typical landscape of the chalk countryside is far behind, indeed the presence of the Winterbourne stream, which we have just crossed, was sufficient to indicate this.

The walk rises steeply from the ford, again as a well-defined track. Scattered houses edge the walk, and in 650 yards from the ford, when the track has levelled out, metalled roads meet the route from the left and ahead. The expanse of common grassland to the right is North Heath, and a maze of unfenced tracks crosses it. Turn right along the southernmost of these, and follow it for about 700 yards. It will then bear sharply left and be joined by several tracks from the right. In almost 200 yards the Blue Boar Inn will be on your right, and just beyond it lies the Wantage to Newbury road and the end of the walk.

# Area 14

**Badbury Hill, Colleymore Farm, Great Coxwell**

**3¾ miles**

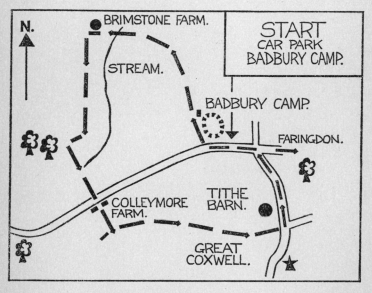

**How to get there:** By road using the B4019 from Faringdon or Highworth. The walk begins at the car park at Badbury camp.

**What to see:** Badbury Camp, the 12th century church at Great Coxwell, the great Tithe Barn also at Great Coxwell, and a considerable variety of undulating countryside, offering extensive views over the upper Thames valley and the Vale of the White Horse.

The walk begins at the car park at Badbury Hill, an area of outstanding countryside owned by the National Trust.

The car park is just over two miles from Faringdon on the B4019, on the right-hand side of the road.

At the car park, the extensive camp is on your right and is well worth close examination. The whole area is in deep woodland, as is the first part of the walk. Leave the car park continuing the line of the entry road keeping the camp to your right. You follow a woodland track which gently winds round to the right and, in two hundred yards, passes an isolated cottage on the right, which backs on to the Camp.

Follow the track which becomes straight for 300 yards, then falls into a narrower footpath and runs steeply downhill. In the distance one can see the buildings of Oldfield Farm which is on the edge of Buscot Park, but the view closer at hand is masked by the woodland through which you are descending.

You leave the woodland suddenly, crossing a gate, and passing underneath power lines. The path carrying on the same line follows a hedgerow on the right. In some 300 yards along the side of the field you will come to a stream which is crossed by a field bridge. Bearing slightly left, again keep the field boundary-hedge on your right. In a couple of hundred yards on the right are the house and buildings of Brimstone Farm.

Turn left on to the farm road, which in about 600 yards, will turn sharply right and left. Badbury Hill rises away to your left while a little further off, to the right, is the larger wooded high ground at Coleshill. Follow the farm road for another 600 yards to the main road at Colleymore Farm. Cross the road and walk straight ahead, keeping the farm house on your right and the farm buildings on your left. At the end of the farmhouse garden the track bears right. At this point take the junction to your left which runs away along the hillside, at first over open fields, then as a wide track between high hedgerows.

In slightly over half a mile you enter the village of Great Coxwell. Should you wish to visit the church, turn right when you come to the main street. The church is 500 yards along on your left. Alternatively, turn left past Court House Farm, and in a few yards on the left you will come to the Great Tithe Barn.

The stone barn is a massive structure and was completed in the mid-13th century by a cell of the Cistercian Order at Beaulieu Abbey. The Barn was bequeathed to the National Trust in 1956 who administer it. It will repay detailed examination. Measuring 152 feet in length and 44 feet in width, the height of the ridge is 48 feet. The interior structure of the roof is particularly interesting and the main load has been carried for 700 years by two rows of slender oak posts, and these principal posts are original.

From the barn, return to the road and turn left along it. The road begins to rise gently and in 900 yards you meet the main Faringdon to Highworth road. This is an old coaching turnpike road. Turn left along it. In 100 yards on the right you will find one of the original milestones, which not only tells you the distance to Faringdon and Highworth, but also tells the traveller how far he is from London. Continue along the road for 300 yards and the entrance to the car park at Badbury Camp will appear on your right.

# Area 15

**Faringdon, Wadley, Littleworth, Faringdon Folly**

**2 miles and 5 miles**

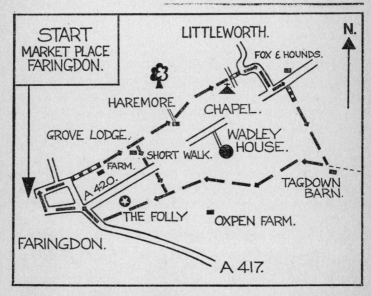

**How to get there:** By road or bus to Faringdon. There is usually ample free parking space in the Market Place, where the walks begin.

**Refreshments: The Bell** or the **Crown** in Faringdon Market or the **Fox and Hounds** at Littleworth.

**What to see:** The old-world Cotswold-style town of Faringdon, and the 13th century parish church. Folly Hill, with Lord Berners' Folly in the centre of trees on the summit.

**The 2 mile walk** begins in Faringdon market place. Walk

gently uphill towards the church. At the **Salutation Hotel** follow the road round to the right. Pass the Radcot road which leaves Faringdon to the left and walk straight on for a few yards. The metalled road will turn sharply right, but carrying on the line which you have walked, is a stone-surfaced bridleway, Still running gently uphill.

In 400 yards from the metalled road the bridlepath passes beside a farm, then having degenerated to a footpath passes along the top slope of a field. Keep the field boundary to your right and the downhill slope to the left. In some 600 yards you will come to a small cottage on the right, called Grove Lodge.

The 2 mile walk passes the cottage, and immediately after it, turns right. (For the 5 mile walk see continuation route from Grove Lodge). Keeping the hedgerow to your right, the footpath runs sharply uphill for almost 300 yards to the A420 which you will need to cross with extreme care. The continuation of the footpath is across the road and slightly to the left, and passes through a metal gate from the roadside. Follow the track which winds gently round to the right, keeping the eminence of Folly Hill to your right, for a further 300 yards. You will come to a signpost indicating footpaths to both left and right. Turn right and proceed up the slope to Folly Hill. From this footpath there are excellent views to be had over the Vale of the White Horse as far as the Berkshire Downs.

You will find that one footpath passes right over the hill passing the Folly which is on your right, another encircles the summit of Folly Hill, with conveniently spaced seats so that one may admire the view in all directions. (5 mile route joins the walk here.)

Continue downhill from the Folly towards Faringdon. The footpath very soon turns into a narrow lane running between walls. In some 500 yards from the Folly you will come to the A417 Faringdon to Wantage road. Turn right along the raised footpath which runs beside it, to its junction with the Oxford road.

At the Oxford road turn left at the Folly Inn and walk downhill along London Street. In 400 yards you will find the market place on the right where the walk ends.


**5 mile walk**

Follow the 2 mile walk from Faringdon market place as far as Grove Lodge. At Grove Lodge, where the 2 mile walk turns right, carry straight on. You will walk (along the left-hand edge of a pasture) roughly parallel with the main Oxford road, which will be away to your right. Haremoor Farm lies ahead of you and the footpath passes to the left of the buildings. Downhill to your left is the considerable oak wood, called Haremoor Wood, lying in a slight re-entrant of the limestone ridge.

From Haremoor Farm the walk proceeds in the same direction, but the going may be hard in wet weather conditions as the footpath has been partly ploughed-out. From the farm buildings keep the boundary fence to your right and aim for the metal gate a hundred yards along the field. Cross the gate. You will now find yourself in an arable field. Keep going in the same general line. On the skyline are two isolated trees and one truncated tree. The path passes just to the right of them.

Very soon the village of Littleworth comes into sight. Prominent on the outskirts of the village is a small and characteristic chapel. The footpath passes into the village just to the left of the chapel and crosses a stile on to a track. Turn right along the track then quickly left. Within a few yards you come to a metal gate. Passing through it, turn right on to the road and walk up the village street.

In 500 yards you join the main Oxford to Faringdon road. Turn left along the footpath beside the road. Ahead you will see the Fox and Hounds Inn, on the left. A few yards short of the inn a track turns right, off the road, and the walk follows the track which becomes a footpath in due course. As a footpath the walk follows a hedgerow to the left and you will come to a prominent hedge ahead of you.